Food, Foretelling, Followers, and Fulfillment

Jesus on His Way to Jerusalem

Cycle B Sermons for
Proper 14 Through Proper 22
Based on the Gospel Texts

Rick McCracken-Bennett

CSS Publishing Company
Lima, Ohio

FOOD, FORETELLING, FOLLOWERS, AND FULFILLMENT

FIRST EDITION
Copyright © 2014
by CSS Publishing Co., Inc.

Library of Congress Cataloging-in-Publication Data

McCracken-Bennett, Rick.
    Food, foretelling, followers, and fulfillment : Jesus on his way to Jerusalem : cycle B sermons for Proper 14 through Proper 22, based on the gospel texts / Rick McCracken-Bennett. -- FIRST EDITION.
        pages cm
    ISBN 0-7880-2783-2 (alk. paper)
    1. Bible. Mark--Sermons. 2. Bible. John--Sermons. 3. Pentecost--Sermons. 4. Common lectionary (1992). Year B. I. Title.

    BS2585.54.M38   2014
    252'64--dc23
                                                    2013047994

For more information about CSS Publishing Company resources, visit our website at www.csspub.com, email us at csr@csspub.com, or call (800) 241-4056.

e-book:
ISBN-13: 978-0-7880-2784-0
ISBN-10: 0-7880-2784-0

ISBN-13: 978-0-7880-2783-3
ISBN-10: 0-7880-2783-2   PRINTED IN USA

*This book is dedicated
to past and present members
of All Saints Episcopal Church, New Albany, Ohio.
We created something very special together —
keep it going!*

Table of Contents

Proper 14   7
Pentecost 11
Ordinary Time 19
Am I Eating Manna or Bread from Heaven?
John 6:35, 41-51

Proper 15   15
Pentecost 12
Ordinary Time 20
Who Do You Think He Is?
John 6:51-58

Proper 16   23
Pentecost 13
Ordinary Time 21
Just Who Does This Guy Think He Is?
John 6:56-69

Proper 17   31
Pentecost 14
Ordinary Time 22
Garbage in… Garbage Out or You Are What You Eat
Mark 7:1-8, 14-15, 21-23

Proper 18   39
Pentecost 15
Ordinary Time 23
Who Does Jesus Belong to Anyway?
Mark 7:24-37

Proper 19   47
Pentecost 16
Ordinary Time 24
    Six Days to Make a Decision for Christ
    Mark 8:27-38

Proper 20   55
Pentecost 17
Ordinary Time 25
    Speaking Truth to Power and Hope to the Powerless
    Mark 9:30-37

Proper 21   61
Pentecost 18
Ordinary Time 26
    Gouge-Your-Eye-Out Sunday
    Mark 9:38-50

Proper 22   69
Pentecost 19
Ordinary Time 27
    And They Lived Happily Ever After… or Did They?
    Mark 10:2-16

Proper 14
Pentecost 11
Ordinary Time 19
John 6:35, 41-51

Jesus said to them, "I am the bread of life. Whoever comes to me will never be hungry, and whoever believes in me will never be thirsty.... Then the Jews began to complain about him because he said, "I am the bread that came down from heaven." They were saying, "Is not this Jesus, the son of Joseph, whose father and mother we know? How can he now say, 'I have come down from heaven'?" Jesus answered them, "Do not complain among yourselves. No one can come to me unless drawn by the Father who sent me; and I will raise that person up on the last day. It is written in the prophets, 'And they shall all be taught by God.' Everyone who has heard and learned from the Father comes to me. Not that anyone has seen the Father except the one who is from God; he has seen the Father. Very truly, I tell you, whoever believes has eternal life. I am the bread of life. Your ancestors ate the manna in the wilderness, and they died. This is the bread that comes down from heaven, so that one may eat of it and not die. I am the living bread that came down from heaven. Whoever eats of this bread will live forever; and the bread that I will give for the life of the world is my flesh."

Am I Eating Manna or Bread from Heaven?

When I was very young, being reared in another denomination, my mother and I, for reasons I cannot remember, were at church together without the rest of the family. In my memory it was evening; also for reasons I cannot remember. What I do recall is that my mother had a very traumatic experience at that service of Holy Eucharist.

We were seated in back instead of in our customary pew halfway up on the left side of the sanctuary and so were among the last to receive communion. We followed the instructions of the ushers and began to solemnly walk up the aisle, hands folded in prayer. When we finally got to the communion rail we knelt and waited for the priest to come and put the host, the bread, on our tongues. This was, as I said, quite some time ago. I received first by virtue of the priest traveling from our right to our left. My mother was next and that's when it happened. The priest missed her tongue. Or maybe she closed her mouth too soon. We'll never know. But the host missed her and the paten that the server had dutifully held underneath her chin, and landed on the floor. All manner of things began to happen at once. The priest called for a purificator and stopped everything to take care lest a single molecule of the bread remained to be trampled underfoot. My mom and I didn't know what to do so we just went back to our pew and knelt down. That's when I saw that she was crying. Weeping actually. Sobbing like I had never seen before. I tried to help but she refused to be consoled.

The priest, after his cleaning duties were complete and he had finished communing the rest of the congregation, came back to my mother and offered her communion. She did not look him in the eye but bowed her head and quietly said "No." He tried to convince her that it was all right, and she should not neglect this opportunity to take Holy Communion but she shook her head again, sniffed, turned her head to blow her nose and never looked back at him. I shrugged my shoulders, the priest shrugged back, and he left.

After church and while we were on our way home I asked her why she didn't take communion when it was later offered. She replied that she had desecrated the sacrament and was thus unworthy to receive it until she could go to confession. I suppose that the next Saturday afternoon when we all dutifully filed into that darkened sanctuary to confess our sins, she confessed her "sin" of desecration. I hope the priest set her straight but I never asked and she never offered to tell me, afraid perhaps, that revealing something said in confession might also result in a sin.

I don't share this story lightly and I hope that I have not told it in such a way that you think I'm making fun of my mother or the practice of communion in this church. I share it to give an example about how seriously some people take the sacrament of Holy Eucharist. And, though not quite to the same degree, I include myself in this group.

If you have been following some of the discussions about communion in our denomination you have no doubt read about the arguments regarding what has become known as "open table." That is, should the Lord's Supper be open to anyone and everyone who presents their outstretched hand to the priest regardless of whether or not they have been baptized. There are thoughtful people on both sides of this discussion and I'll share with you where I stand before I'm finished.

The official stance in the Episcopal church as stated in the canons is that communion is open to all baptized Christians regardless of where they were baptized. (As long as the Trinitarian formula was used: I baptize you in the name of *the Father, the Son, and the Holy Spirit*.) It is stated this way in our canons (specifically Canon 1.17.7) "No unbaptized person shall be eligible to receive Holy Communion in this church."

So most of the time you will hear the invitation given something like this: "All baptized Christians are welcome to receive communion at this table." Then a word or two of instructions are given before the service continues. On the surface this sounds very open and inclusive.

I have, however, adopted a slightly different wording, but with a significantly different meaning. I say, "All are welcome to receive communion at this table." I came to this understanding and practice this way. Early on in the planting of this church I was still so naïve to think that everyone and their brother were baptized. In the rural congregations in which I had previously served, this was the case. Even crusty, old curmudgeons who only showed up on Christmas and Easter had, in the far distant past, received the sacrament of Baptism. And as yet, a decade and a half ago, I had not heard of this period in history being called the post-Christian era. So I merrily went on my way until one day when a man about my own age came up to me after church one Sunday when we had celebrated a baptism and asked if he too could be baptized. I was shocked. I shouldn't have been, but I was. I composed myself and asked him what brought him to this place in his life and he said that ever since he came here and received communion Sunday after Sunday that a desire to dedicate his life to God had grown and that the best way he knew how was to make his baptismal promises and be baptized.

That, and many other instances like it, is why I choose to welcome all to the table and not make any exceptions. I am not a great theologian. I cannot wax eloquent about the theological rightness or wrongness of my practice. I can only tell you that I do what my heart tells me is right to do.

So what about children? Traditions vary but I like what I heard an old priest say once. (Now I say "old" but he was probably younger than I am now!) He said that it was his wish that every child would have a memory of *always* being welcomed at the Lord's table. I mentioned this to my mother one day. Her response was that a child would not understand what was going on. I agreed that this was likely to be the case. Then I asked my mom to explain what was going on in the bread and in the wine and she was stymied. Which brings up the question, do I need to intellectually understand what is happening to the bread and wine in the Eucharist in order for the sacrament to be valid or effective? If that were the case we wouldn't baptize babies or anoint a comatose patient since they would not be aware of what was happening. Again, people can differ on this, but I think God is able to work wonders in our souls whether or not we're aware of it, and whether or not our intellectual understanding is correct or not.

Let me be clear; I respect our parents who have chosen to bring their children forward for a blessing instead of taking the bread and the wine. I get it. I suspect that in doing so their child will be apt to ask questions about what's going on and will be able to express, in time, what his/her desire is regarding Holy Communion.

Whatever your intellectual, emotional, theological, or spiritual experiences with Holy Communion, may this sacrament continue to be for you a holy, life-giving, mysterious magnet drawing you ever closer to the love of God who sent his son that we might never be hungry nor thirsty, this day, tomorrow, and forever and ever. Amen.

Proper 15
Pentecost 12
Ordinary Time 20
John 6:51-58

I am the living bread that came down from heaven. Whoever eats of this bread will live forever; and the bread that I will give for the life of the world is my flesh." The Jews then disputed among themselves, saying, "How can this man give us his flesh to eat?" So Jesus said to them, "Very truly, I tell you, unless you eat the flesh of the Son of Man and drink his blood, you have no life in you. Those who eat my flesh and drink my blood have eternal life, and I will raise them up on the last day; for my flesh is true food and my blood is true drink. Those who eat my flesh and drink my blood abide in me, and I in them. Just as the living Father sent me, and I live because of the Father, so whoever eats me will live because of me. This is the bread that came down from heaven, not like that which your ancestors ate, and they died. But the one who eats this bread will live forever."

Who Do You Think He Is?

A number of years ago a priest, who happened to be a woman, moved to a more conservative diocese after her husband, who also was a priest, died. I knew Mary (not her real name). She was a wonderful priest, loved by her congregation. We were all sad to see her leave our area.

After she got settled she scheduled an appointment with the local bishop. After a little polite chitchat she began the conversation by telling him when she had been ordained, who ordained her, where she had served as a priest, and what kind of work she did in southern Ohio. She concluded by offering to serve in any capacity that he, the bishop, thought might be appropriate.

When she paused, I was told, thirdhand, so the exact words may have been lost in translation though the meaning is crystal clear, the bishop leaned over his desk, stared at her and said, "I don't know what you think happened when your bishop placed his hands on your head, but I can tell you... nothing happened." In other words, she, in his opinion, was not a priest, because women cannot become priests in his theological framework, and even if they *think* they've been ordained, it was nothing but a day to play dress-up, to pretend that God had changed her through the laying on of hands. She was not, in his opinion, who she thought she was. Her opinion of herself was scandalous in his mind. How dare she come in there and presume to call herself a priest when

17

the Bible, in his opinion, precludes persons of that gender from being one? In his mind, she was not who she thought she was.

Recently I was preparing for a class in which we would discuss the differences between the Episcopal church and the various denominations that so many of us come from. These are always lively conversations; ones that I especially enjoy, having, at one time, served in another franchise of the Christian church.

The question always comes up, *What do we believe happens to the bread and the wine during Holy Eucharist?* They're not asking what do you do with the leftovers. They are asking, "What, if anything, changes?" What happens? Is it a memorial meal, a remembering of the Last Supper? How is it that the bread and wine are suddenly different than the bread and wine I served at dinner last evening? Or for that matter, how is the bread and wine different than they were just a few minutes before? Or, in the words of our gospel today, "How can this man give us his flesh to eat?" (John 6:52).

In my research I came across the argument that Episcopal priests cannot change the bread and the wine into the body and blood of Christ (never mind that it is God who is doing the changing here). They can't change it because they do not have the authority to change it; to consecrate the bread and wine. It got a little more technical than that, more than we have time for, and probably more than you have patience for. I read as much of this man's snotty essay as I could stand and then decided to agree to disagree.

I can tell you what I believe and that is that the bread and the wine are turned into the body and blood of Christ. I have to stop there, because I don't *how* that comes about. Certainly it does not happen because of any holiness on my part, and it is not because I say certain magical words.

A quick aside here: Do you know where the magicians' words: *hocus pocus* come from? The legend goes, and it may or may not be entirely true, that hocus pocus is a corruption of the words that a priest used to utter in Latin, with his back to the people: *hoc est corpus meum*, "This is my body," and because the congregation couldn't hear clearly, and because some regarded the words themselves as having magical powers, magicians began to use them. I'm reminded of a cartoon where the minister in the pulpit asks the question, "Is something wrong with the sound system?" to which the congregation replied, "And also with you." Sometimes we hear only what we *think* we hear. As I said, some, perhaps many, disagree with that explanation, but it's a great story and besides, in the end, what difference does it make?

What I do know is that Holy Communion is a sacrament, and as a sacrament, it is, according to our catechism in the *Book of Common Prayer* (p. 857) an outward and visible sign of inward and spiritual grace. In other words, just like in baptism, the water poured over a person's head or into which a person is submerged, is a sign that the person has been spiritually changed from the inside out, and they have died with Christ so that they might rise with him. The bread and the wine, changed into Christ's body and blood, become for us a sign of what Christ is doing inside us, in our very souls.

Years ago there was a wonderful family who had a daughter named Georgina. She was little, she was very young, maybe three or four. Every time she came up with her parents in the communion line, they would gently restrain her from receiving the bread from me and asked that I say a blessing over her instead. When I asked why, since, as a church, we don't restrict communion to those of age, so to speak, they said that she was too young. She wouldn't understand it anymore than if it were a snack at coffee hour.

So on it went, Sunday after Sunday, they would come up, Georgina would struggle to get her hands on the bread, and her parents would lovingly ask me to give her a blessing. One Sunday, I'll never forget, we were worshiping in the high school in those days, Georgina broke loose from her parents, and came all the way down the aisle between the two rows of other communicants, looked at me with those big, blue eyes and held up her hand. She stopped right there in front of me and just stared up and waited. I looked back at her parents and they both smiled and nodded. She apparently knew more than we thought. Somewhere in her heart and soul this little girl knew that it was the most important thing she could do that Sunday, to break free of her mooring, come to the head of the line, and hold her hands outstretched and up to me, and receive the body and blood of Christ.

Of course, this isn't confined to children. One of our adults who attends church every now and then came up to me for communion one Sunday and just looked different. I can't describe it any better than that... she just looked different to me. After church I had a chance to ask her what was going on and she said that during the Eucharistic Prayer that Sunday she suddenly "got it." She understood something of the nature of what she was doing on a much deeper level than she had previously.

I could give you many more examples of experiences I've had as you come up for Holy Communion. It is as if some of that inward grace leaks out, sometimes so much that if we have the eyes to see and the ears to hear we would experience it. Many of you, like the woman I mentioned a minute ago, look different to me sometimes. You might look hungry or anxious to receive the bread and wine. Others have said to me, I don't know what happened today, but I suddenly experienced the bread and wine as something very sacred, holy, as the very body and blood of Jesus Christ. I would dare anyone to say to these people that no matter what they *think* happens, or what they *think* changes in the bread and the wine, that nothing actually happens. Nothing changes. I dare them.

I once knew of a recovering alcoholic priest who was asked how he dared to drink the communion wine. Didn't that break his sobriety? Wasn't that cheating? Didn't he risk relapsing back to his drug of choice? He replied that for a year or two after getting sober he used grape juice. But, for him, communion was no longer simply wine in the same way as dinner wine. It had, in fact, been changed into the body and blood of Christ, and that he believed that Christ was not about to send him spinning back into that hell on earth that he had clawed his way out of. He has been sober now for over 35 years. Still he added, the moment he stopped believing that the wine was no longer just wine, he would instantly stop drinking it, and if grape juice were available he would take that instead. I dare anyone to tell this priest that the bread and the wine are simply bread and wine, no different than when they were brought to the table a few minutes before. For this priest, the distinction is important. Actually, it is critically important. In fact, his very life depends upon taking communion with that belief intact.

So today, let's be mindful of what we're doing here. Let's look upon this sacrament with wonder and awe, and bring our sins, and even our doubts, and behold the very presence of Jesus in this humble sacrament of bread and wine, of the body and blood of our Lord Jesus Christ. Amen.

Proper 16
Pentecost 13
Ordinary Time 21
John 6:56-69

Those who eat my flesh and drink my blood abide in me, and I in them. Just as the living Father sent me, and I live because of the Father, so whoever eats me will live because of me. This is the bread that came down from heaven, not like that which your ancestors ate, and they died. But the one who eats this bread will live forever." He said these things while he was teaching in the synagogue at Capernaum. When many of his disciples heard it, they said, "This teaching is difficult; who can accept it?" But Jesus, being aware that his disciples were complaining about it, said to them, "Does this offend you? Then what if you were to see the Son of Man ascending to where he was before? It is the spirit that gives life; the flesh is useless. The words that I have spoken to you are spirit and life. But among you there are some who do not believe." For Jesus knew from the first who were the ones that did not believe, and who was the one that would betray him. And he said, "For this reason I have told you that no one can come to me unless it is granted by the Father." Because of this many of his disciples turned back and no longer went about with him. So Jesus asked the twelve, "Do you also wish to go away?" Simon Peter answered him, "Lord, to whom can we go? You have the words of eternal life. We have come to believe and know that you are the Holy One of God."

Just Who Does This Guy Think He Is?

"I think he's speaking in metaphors," Stephen said.

"I don't care if he's speaking in Chicago, he's getting downright spooky," replied Andrew, not one of the twelve.

Jesus had been speaking for what seemed to be days to a crowd made up of his disciples, hundreds of them, as well as his twelve nearest and dearest disciples. Bread, bread, and bread... it was all he seemed to be talking about. It was enough to make a person hungry. They all knew stories about how God provided for his people who had escaped slavery in Egypt and were in the desert making their way to a land that God promised them. They knew about God giving them bread from heaven. Manna, they called it. Which, by the way, was their word for "what is it?" For those wanderers didn't know what that white, crumbly stuff was that fell like dew each morning.

These contemporary disciples of Jesus understood *that* story, and the bread that God provided for them. But this? This was almost blasphemy. Perhaps it *was* blasphemy. Referring to himself as the bread come down from heaven. The people began to grumble. You can imagine how they whispered to each other.

What does he mean when he says he is the living bread come down from heaven?

Another said, *Yeah, and that eating this bread means we'll never go hungry again. Who does he think he is? Who does he think he's kidding?*

Some of the religious leaders, some of the powers that be, began to complain about him. And that was bad… it was very bad. Already, the most astute among the crowd knew that this was not going to end well. These religious authorities thought it was ludicrous that he would refer to himself as the bread that came down from heaven. It seemed so obvious to them that this was impossible. After all, they knew his father, Joseph and they knew his mother, Mary. He was a man and not some God who came floating down from the sky. It made absolutely no sense to them to think that Jesus had, in some way, come down from heaven and that God had sent him! No way.

And it got worse. Jesus upped the ante and proclaimed to them that it was God's will that everyone who sees him, Jesus, and believes in him, will have eternal life, and will be raised on the last day. The grumbling got louder. He looked the powers that be straight in the eye and told them that no one has ever seen God *except him*! Then he began to tell them some things that made some of them kind of squeamish.

He told them that he is the living bread and that anyone who eats this bread will live forever. Some were so turned off that they didn't even hear him say that the bread that he would give was his flesh, for the life of the world.

Stephen looked at Andrew, "See, I told you he was speaking in metaphors. He doesn't expect us to eat his flesh exactly."

"Then what *does* he mean?" Andrew retorted.

"I'm not sure, but I do believe that this is something we can not and should not take literally."

They turned their attention back to Jesus as he then told them that those who ate this bread and drank his blood would abide in him. Andrew said, "Abide? Abide? If he means to put up with him, or to tolerate him and his teaching, I get it. But it sure as heck is getting hard to stomach." Andrew and the religious authorities weren't the only ones grumbling, others of his followers were saying to each other that his teachings were too difficult to accept.

Why wasn't he telling them nice stories like he used to, about sheep or the lilies of the field? Those were pleasant. Those were stories that everyone could appreciate. But this? Whew!

Jesus knew what they were thinking; he always seemed to know what people were thinking. Not because he was some kind of mind reader, but because he was so darn good at reading people. He looked at them and said, "So... does this offend you? Well then, what would you think if you saw me ascending back to heaven? You may be offended by what I've been saying, but the words I've spoken are spirit and life. Still (and then he looked them all over) still there are some of you who do not believe." And he wasn't only referring to Judas who he knew was going to betray him, he was talking about many who had been following him.

He went on, "This is the very reason I have told you that no one can come to me unless the Father grants it."

Well that was it! Many of the disciples couldn't take it anymore. If they took his words literally they couldn't stomach it. And they couldn't see past those words to the truth that Jesus was trying to convey. Disciples stood and walked away. The crowd got smaller, quite a bit smaller. And eventually they got quieter, quite a bit quieter.

Jesus watched them leave and then turned back to the twelve disciples who had been with him from the beginning.

"How about you? Are you going to go away too? Do you find my words offensive? Do you think I'm losing my mind, and what I'm teaching is pure heresy?"

The twelve were quiet for some time. Finally Peter spoke up. It was always Peter. The other eleven just rolled their eyes. Peter was, they thought, about to put his foot in his mouth… again! But he surprised them. "Lord, where else would we go? Even though we don't understand exactly what you're saying, there is something there; your very words are words of eternal life. There's no one else like you. Never has been, and I believe, never will be." Peter looked around at the others to see if they were with him and they nodded. Then he said, "Jesus, in the time we've been with you, we have come to believe and know that you are God's holy one." And the rest of the twelve nodded again.

It would be a long time before they understood all that Jesus was teaching. And they would get it wrong some of the time, especially that eager, impetuous Simon Peter. But they hung in there with him. They pondered his words; they asked Jesus and each other what he meant below the surface of the literal words. Like rabbis in later years they would literally chew on his words.

Like Christians in the centuries since, they would scour the Bible for other passages in the Hebrew scriptures that seemed to point to Jesus and his redeeming work and try to put it all together. Yet there was always something that seemed just outside their grasp, not so far that they were tempted to give up, turn back, and no longer go about with Jesus, but, interestingly enough, something mysterious that actually drew them closer to Jesus, closer to God.

It is that mystery that still draws people from all walks of life to Jesus, the living bread come down from heaven, Jesus who abides in us even as we abide in him. Jesus, whose words are spirit and truth; life-giving, eternal life-giving words of truth. Amen.

Proper 17
Pentecost 14
Ordinary Time 22
Mark 7:1-8, 14-15, 21-23

Now when the Pharisees and some of the scribes who had come from Jerusalem gathered around him, they noticed that some of his disciples were eating with defiled hands, that is, without washing them. (For the Pharisees, and all the Jews, do not eat unless they thoroughly wash their hands, thus observing the tradition of the elders; and they do not eat anything from the market unless they wash it; and there are also many other traditions that they observe, the washing of cups, pots, and bronze kettles.) So the Pharisees and the scribes asked him, "Why do your disciples not live according to the tradition of the elders, but eat with defiled hands?" He said to them, "Isaiah prophesied rightly about you hypocrites, as it is written, 'This people honors me with their lips, but their hearts are far from me; in vain do they worship me, teaching human precepts as doctrines.' You abandon the commandment of God and hold to human tradition...." Then he called the crowd again and said to them, "Listen to me, all of you, and understand: there is nothing outside a person that by going in can defile, but the things that come out are what defile...." "For it is from within, from the human heart, that evil intentions come: fornication, theft, murder, adultery, avarice, wickedness, deceit, licentiousness, envy, slander, pride, folly. All these evil things come from within, and they defile a person."

Garbage in... Garbage Out
or You Are What You Eat

The Pharisees were grumbling — doesn't it seem like they were always grumbling? Of all the things they could be concerned about, they were upset that Jesus' disciples weren't washing their hands before they ate. As I read this passage over earlier in the week I could hear my mom asking me and my brother and sisters before a meal, "Did you wash your hands?" This was an appropriate question for parents trying to teach their children good hygiene. But, at first glance, a strange concern for a religious leader, don't you think? It wasn't like they were afraid that these guys would get their food all germy, they were concerned that the disciples were breaking one of their rules; one of the traditions of their elders.

It was a good way to take a pot-shot at Jesus. *See, he couldn't possibly be who people say he is because either he doesn't know the rules of the game, or he chooses to ignore them.* These religious powers that be were claiming that everyone had to follow human precepts in order to be acceptable to God. The Pharisees were preaching that, like computer programmers of today, "Garbage in, garbage out." Or, in the words of nutritionists, "You are what you eat." Jesus uses their rigid interpretation of these human rules to teach the crowd that "there is nothing outside a person that by go-

33

ing in can defile, but the things that come out are what defile" (Mark 7:15).

Then he recites a list of nasty sins that can come out of a person's heart and defile a person. Even if this is true, what goes into a person does not define what comes out of a person in terms of their behavior, I think it's still safe to say, we ought to hedge our bets and make certain that good things go into a person, so we can expect that good things are going to come out.

I'd be the last person to give anyone dietary advice; what foods are good, and will produce good health, and what foods are bad for you. A friend once said to me, pardon the expression, we shouldn't eat crap, and we all know what crap is. Likewise, we need to be careful about what we hear and see, what values we're exposed to, what values are crap, lest the wrong things come bursting out of our hearts.

Over the years I've belonged to a couple of different service organizations, primarily the Kiwanis Club and the Lions Club. Both of them have core values that they expect their members to live by.

Six permanent Objects of Kiwanis International were approved by Kiwanis club delegates at the 1924 Kiwanis International Convention in Denver, Colorado. Through the decades, they have remained unchanged.

• To give primacy to the human and spiritual rather than to the material values of life.

• To encourage the daily living of the golden rule in all human relationships.

• To promote the adoption and the application of higher social, business, and professional standards.

• To develop, by precept and example, a more intelligent, aggressive, and serviceable citizenship.

• To provide, through Kiwanis clubs, a practical means to

form enduring friendships, to render altruistic service, and to build better communities.

• To cooperate in creating and maintaining that sound public opinion and high idealism which make possible the increase of righteousness, justice, patriotism, and goodwill.[1]

The Lions Club holds as its core values that of *integrity, accountability, teamwork,* and *excellence.*[2] Along with their motto, *We Serve,* these values become a part of every aspect of the club and all members are expected to adhere to them.

I must have learned the Boy Scout law when I was eleven or twelve years old. And I can still recite it pretty much word for word. In fact, I do not even have to look it up! A scout is loyal, helpful, friendly, courteous, kind, obedient, cheerful, thrifty, brave, clean, and reverent. These, along with the Boy Scout slogan, "Do a good turn daily" do much to form the moral lives of young men.[3]

When I began working in a hospital some time ago I was encouraged to read all of the so-called positive thinking books. The idea was that there was nothing I couldn't accomplish if I kept a positive attitude. I learned to repeat over and over, positive affirmations. And I did... over and over and over. I suppose that was more helpful than repeating negative statements like, I'm too stupid, too slow, I'm too inexperienced. Over time I stopped using these affirmations. I'm not sure why, I just stopped thinking about them. However, I did begin to pick up some different ones that have become increasingly helpful and very much a part of my spiritual disciplines. These mantras are often verses of scripture, most often from one of the psalms.

One I turn to most often is from Psalm 51: "Create in me a clean heart, O God, and put a new and right spirit within me" (v. 10). Those words, repeated over and over, often put my mind and my heart back where they belong. In some way I believe this mantra helps to protect me from expressing negative or bad thoughts that I am exposed to day after day.

Lately I have become quite fond of a quote from Julian of Norwich, a very important Christian mystic. She is famously quoted as saying, "All shall be well, and all shall be well, and all manner of things shall be well." On days when I have lost my grip on hope I find myself repeating this mantra throughout the day and even falling asleep to the words. Because I hold those words to be true I am comfortable offering them to people going through difficult times.

Maybe it's my age (seems like I'm saying that more often these days), but I've been thinking about the years of child rearing gone by and the years of grandparenting in my future. I think about what values we tried to instill in our children, and what values we tried *not* to teach. An example of a bad value, in my mind, that I didn't want my kids to acquire, was that they were to win at any cost. Hopefully we don't see much of that in our schools, but in professional sports it's there all the time. Bonuses paid to players who injure an opposing team member are just one example. We sometimes see that "value" lived out in business (remember the movie *Wall Street*?). We often see that "value" expressed in politics… enough said.

A friend confided in me the other day that he lost his job due to corporate downsizing. He had gone through a long period of unemployment before landing this one and I thought he would be devastated to realize that he might have to walk through that desert again. While he was sad and a little scared he didn't seem as crushed as I had expected. I learned why a couple of days later when I spoke with his wife. She said that the core values of the company were the very antithesis of the values that their family lived by and that they were both relieved that the tension between the two value systems was over, even at the cost of his job.

Garbage in, garbage out. You are what you eat. Whatever value software is running in your heart will likely come out in your behavior. So what values do we want to have a place in our children's hearts, or, for that matter, in our own?

Let's just take one and look at how we can instill, or *install* that value in our young people.

Service to others. Every time we do some act of outreach through our church I am thrilled to see that you bring your children along. Yes, perhaps we're trying to remind our kids how fortunate they are, but on a much deeper level, we are teaching them that true meaning in life is found when we serve others and leave behind our me, me, me nature. Remember the Boy Scout slogan: Do a good turn daily. I've said it until I'm blue in the face that what we do here as a church is not about you, and it's not about me, it's about carrying on the mission of Christ and a big chunk of that is service to others.

Well, that's enough for now. I hope though, that we'll all give this a bit of thought today and this week. What values are we doing our best to instill in our kids and grandkids, and in ourselves, so that what comes out of our hearts is loyalty, helpfulness, faithfulness, kindness? You get the idea. No matter what we choose, let's always remember to choose wisely. Amen.

---

1. http://sites.kiwanis.org/Kiwanis/en/discover/ourvalues.aspx.

2. http://www.lionsclubs.org/EN/common/pdfs/lg414.pdf

3. http://usscouts.org/advance/boyscout/bsoathlaw.asp

Proper 18
Pentecost 15
Ordinary Time 23
Mark 7:24-37

From there he set out and went away to the region of Tyre.
He entered a house and did not want anyone to know he
was there. Yet he could not escape notice, but a woman
whose little daughter had an unclean spirit immediately
heard about him, and she came and bowed down at his feet.
Now the woman was a Gentile, of Syrophoenician origin.
She begged him to cast the demon out of her daughter. He
said to her, "Let the children be fed first, for it is not fair to
take the children's food and throw it to the dogs." But she
answered him, "Sir, even the dogs under the table eat the
children's crumbs." Then he said to her, "For saying that,
you may go — the demon has left your daughter." So she
went home, found the child lying on the bed, and the demon
gone. Then he returned from the region of Tyre, and went by
way of Sidon toward the Sea of Galilee, in the region of the
Decapolis. They brought to him a deaf man who had an im-
pediment in his speech; and they begged him to lay his hand
on him. He took him aside in private, away from the crowd,
and put his fingers into his ears, and he spat and touched
his tongue. Then looking up to heaven, he sighed and said to
him, "Ephphatha," that is, "Be opened." And immediately
his ears were opened, his tongue was released, and he spoke
plainly. Then Jesus ordered them to tell no one; but the more
he ordered them, the more zealously they proclaimed it. They
were astounded beyond measure, saying, "He has done ev-
erything well; he even makes the deaf to hear and the mute
to speak."

Who Does Jesus Belong to Anyway?

I don't know why but for the longest time I never thought of Jesus getting tired. Silly of me I suppose, but I kind of thought of him, in the brief time his ministry was going to last, going at it full tilt until the end. Stopping to pray, of course. But not going away, taking a break, not wanting anyone to know he was there. But now I get it.

I was at Wendy's the other day. I was tired. I needed to get away from the phone and the other interruptions and just have some quiet time with this gospel text and my fries. As I approached the line a man waiting to get his food gave me the kind of friendly welcome you usually get from someone you know. I'm usually pretty good with faces and thought that I had met him somewhere but couldn't place him. Turns out that he didn't know me either. He was just being friendly. Long story short, after asking about what I was reading, whether or not I was a pastor, and questions about the Episcopal church, he left. Next time… I'll need to find another place to get away and escape notice. Sometimes a person just needs a break.

Anyway, Jesus flew under the radar to a private house and most likely had just sat down in the BarcaLounger® with his feet up and was sipping some sweetened ice tea when there was a knock on the door. What now? Can't this poor guy catch a break?

In walked a Gentile, a Syrophoenician woman who bowed at his feet. Right away we know that this might not end well. Jews and Syrophoenicians had bad blood going way back. She told Jesus about her beloved daughter and how she had this unclean spirit inside her. Let me say, regardless of what we think of demonic possession, something was obviously desperately wrong with her daughter. Jesus responded to her request like an exhausted person might. Grumpy Jesus said about the nastiest thing he could to this woman. While his attacks on hypocritical religious authorities (and sometimes his own disciples) were often of this nature, Jesus was remarkably patient with the lay people with whom he came into contact. He said, "Let the children be fed first, for it is not fair to take the children's food and throw it to the dogs" (Mark 7:27). Though it's possible that Jesus was pointing to and referring to a domesticated dog lying at his feet, the Hebrews found dogs in general to be utterly disgusting scavengers. So Jesus could have been saying here that a filthy, disgusting dog is more deserving of care than this woman's daughter. It's interesting to note that even the most critical of scripture scholars would agree that Jesus spoke those words since Mark included them even though they did not cast Jesus in the best light.

The woman could have run away in tears. She might have had a shred of dignity left and said, "Thank you, anyway." Instead she stood her ground. Nothing, not even this rude prophet, was going to stand in the way of getting help for her beloved daughter. You recall how she responded to his name calling, "Sir, even the dogs under the table eat the children's crumbs." In other words, I'll gladly take leftovers. In fact, she seemed to be saying with great faith, that leftovers would be enough to make her daughter whole again. And then Jesus, without touching her daughter, without laying his eyes or hands on her, and it seems, without even looking up to heaven to pray, pronounced the woman's daughter healed. And she was.

The Syrophoenician woman's story and Jesus' response reminds me to pray always and not give up hope. It reminds me of the lament psalms in the Hebrew scriptures which have the person asking why God is failing to act and then reminding God of what God's job is, all with faith that the psalmist's request will be honored. I am also reminded that I cannot dictate what kind of healing is to take place. While I may want someone's cancer to go away, or a couple to work out their differences and restore their marriage, the healing that takes place may be subtler. It may be that the ones I'm praying for are handed a closer walk with God or peace. In some cases they may receive the ultimate healing of life forever with God.

It looked like Jesus wasn't going to get much rest in Tyre and so he and his companions packed up and moved on and were, once again, joined by the crowd. On their way some people came up to Jesus and interceded for a fellow who could not speak because he was deaf and had a speech impediment. They begged Jesus to help their poor friend. Jesus took him away in private, which, I think, was a good thing, since the gestures he was going to use to heal this man were disgusting. Tough to stomach, you might say. He put his fingers in the man's ears. So far, so good. But then he spat and touched the guy's tongue. We assume that Jesus didn't just spit like a major league ball player between pitches. He spat on his fingers before touching his tongue. Why? We'll never know but again, it is likely the action he took and not one made up by Mark. Jesus looked up to heaven. Here is the prayer that seemed to be missing in the first healing story, "Be opened." Mark included the words in Jesus' native tongue. We'll never know why he chose to do that. Instantly the man was healed. The gospel reports that he "spoke plainly." I suspect more accurately that the man shouted, "Yahoo!"

Jesus tried to keep everyone quiet about this healing. Again, we don't know why but we can make a couple of educated guesses. Maybe he was still exhausted and was concerned that every sick person in the territory was going to rush over to be healed. Perhaps he did not want his ministry to be about healing but rather about proclaiming and bringing about the reign of God. In the end it did not matter since, despite Jesus' orders, they told the world "he has done everything well; he even makes the deaf to hear and the mute to speak" (Mark 7:37).

In those two stories it is a third party who asked Jesus to help. Same thing with you and me. We are often asked by people to pray for others. In our bulletin we have nearly a hundred names of people who have requested our prayers. And, I know, we all say that we will do just that. But even the most well meaning of us tend to forget over time. So here are a couple of suggestions. When we say that we will pray for someone, make sure we get his or her name. It sounds obvious but I can't tell you how many times I've been asked to pray for someone's relative and failed to get their name. I know that God knows, but I still want the prayer to be personal. Start a prayer journal even it it's on the back of an envelope you keep on your person. If you have a smart phone or tablet there are free prayer apps that can help us remember to pray and remember what we are praying for. Then set aside some time each day to remember them in prayer. Stand in the long line of those who have brought people to Jesus for help, from the Syrophoenician woman to the anonymous folks who brought the deaf man who was unable to speak.

Pray and then let God be God. Let God decide in what form the healing will be. Amen.

Proper 19
Pentecost 16
Ordinary Time 24
Mark 8:27-38

Jesus went on with his disciples to the villages of Caesarea Philippi; and on the way he asked his disciples, "Who do people say that I am?" And they answered him, "John the Baptist; and others, Elijah; and still others, one of the prophets." He asked them, "But who do you say that I am?" Peter answered him, "You are the Messiah." And he sternly ordered them not to tell anyone about him. Then he began to teach them that the Son of Man must undergo great suffering, and be rejected by the elders, the chief priests, and the scribes, and be killed, and after three days rise again. He said all this quite openly. And Peter took him aside and began to rebuke him. But turning and looking at his disciples, he rebuked Peter and said, "Get behind me, Satan! For you are setting your mind not on divine things but on human things." He called the crowd with his disciples, and said to them, "If any want to become my followers, let them deny themselves and take up their cross and follow me. For those who want to save their life will lose it, and those who lose their life for my sake, and for the sake of the gospel, will save it. For what will it profit them to gain the whole world and forfeit their life? Indeed, what can they give in return for their life? Those who are ashamed of me and of my words in this adulterous and sinful generation, of them the Son of Man will also be ashamed when he comes in the glory of his Father with the holy angels."

Six Days to Make
a Decision for Christ

Whether they knew it or not, the disciples were about to begin an intensive seminar on discipleship. It was time for Boot Camp. As Mark implied in his repetitive use of the word, "immediately," there was an urgency about Jesus and he was running out of time before he handed over the reigns to the twelve. He needed to know what they understood and what they didn't; how much remediation was this bunch going to require? Were they able to see beneath the signs that he had performed to the deeper, richer message? When he healed the blind did they realize, for instance, that there were different kinds of blindness? Did they understand that they are sometimes blind? It was time to heat things up.

Jesus began by asking an easy question. A safe question. "Who do people say that I am?" (Mark 8:27b). What are they saying out there? What do you hear as you serve food to the hungry? They answered that some are still a bit confused. Some thought he was John the Baptist; others, that he was Elijah. Others thought that he was one of the other prophets of old. You can almost see Jesus nodding in agreement. Just like he thought. That was the easy question and they aced it. But before they could pat each other on the back he got right to the point, "But who do you say that I am?" (Mark 8:29a). Peter piped up and answered that he is the Messiah. Jesus then ordered them to tell no one. Let them go on believing for now that he is John or Elijah but don't correct them.

Then Jesus took them to school and showed them why. I thought of this passage the other day when I was in a doctor's exam room. Two medical students, one obviously a year or two further along than the other, took turns asking me questions. This went on for some time. They left after telling me that they would consult with the "real" doctor and that they'd all be back to discuss what they would recommend. The three of them returned five or ten minutes later and after some chitchat the doctor asked his students what they had learned about me. The younger, less experienced one gave a run-down of my symptoms and when he was finished the more seasoned student, already an MD, gave the diagnosis. It was then that the "real" doctor took them to school. He didn't agree with the diagnosis and while he did agree with one of the medicines that the students recommended, he said to the older student regarding the other medicine, "You can prescribe that in somebody else's practice but not in mine. Why? It doesn't work." The student doctors were taken aback, embarrassed but held up remarkably well as he continue to "school" them. I'll bet that Peter felt pretty much the same way in the face of Jesus taking him to school.

"Who do you say that I am?" Jesus asked and Peter answered correctly. Well, sort of correctly. He held the common belief that the Messiah would be king over Israel and lead, most likely, a revolt against their oppressors; in this case, the Romans. But Jesus talked of a whole different understanding of what would be the Messiah's life and ministry when he spoke of suffering, rejection by the religious authorities, and being killed, and after three days rising from the dead (Mark 8:31).

Here's where Peter should have kept his mouth shut

— really. He needed to sit back and ponder Jesus' words. He needed to consult with some of the other disciples. He needed to search the scriptures to see if any of the predictions of a messiah lined up with this frightening description from Jesus. But no, he took Jesus aside and tried to take *Jesus* to school. He barely got started when Jesus unleashed an explosive rebuke of his own. He seemed to be saying to Peter that, though Peter might have considered his position in this disciple band to be that of a leader, Jesus needed to pull him out of the leadership position, put him behind himself once again, and remind him that he was not ready to assume leadership just yet.

Peter's mind was not on divine things, heavenly things, kingdom things; he was instead looking at messiahship from a purely human point of view. Peter meant well. He didn't want his beloved teacher to suffer and die. But in saying this he told Jesus in no uncertain terms that he didn't understand the mission and wasn't yet ready to lead.

Jesus broke up his one-on-one with Peter and called the crowd together. Had they heard the confrontation? Had they sensed the anger in Jesus' voice even if they couldn't quite make out the words? We don't know. But regardless he had something to tell the twelve and the others in the crowd.

The verbs used here in his speech to the crowd are important. Listen to them with only an additional word or two. *Deny yourself. Take up your cross. To save your life you must lose it. Lose your life* (for the right reasons, that is, for Jesus' sake and the sake of the gospel) *and you will save it.* And going back to his theme of heavenly versus earthly things he cautioned them that *it would not profit them to gain the world if it caused them to forfeit their lives. And finally, if they are ashamed of him and of his words Jesus will be ashamed of them when he returns.*

I can see the look on the faces of the disciples and the crowd. Can you? They have the look of my young medical students. They look like an employee being justly reprimanded by their supervisor. It is the look on a college student's face after they answer a professor's question incorrectly but with the bravado of someone who doesn't yet know what she doesn't know and is put in her place.

Following this event the gospel writer we call Mark does something uncharacteristic. Instead of telling us that Jesus *immediately* went to do this or that, he took a six-day break from the narrative. Again, we don't know why but let me propose a possible reason.

After such harsh words to Peter, and describing the sacrifices that would have to be made by anyone wanting to follow him, Jesus gave them a little time off to process what he had taught them to this point. Peter probably needed to lick his wounds and put himself back together to begin to save face with the others. Members of the crowd had some decisions to make. They had probably heard what Jesus had taught the disciples about his upcoming suffering, rejection, assassination, and rising again as well as the job description Jesus laid out for them. And they needed to think about this — pray about this. The people in the crowd had to ask themselves if continuing to follow Jesus would be dangerous to their health and if they were willing to sacrifice it all to continue on this path.

You and I have six days before we will all meet again. You've heard the words of Jesus just like the disciples and the crowd did. It is likely that we weren't surprised by Jesus telling them that things were not going to look like they were going to end well; but his charge to the crowd and us about denying ourselves, our feeble attempts to save our lives resulting in losing them, might bring us up short. And they should!

Take the next six days if you dare, to consider your behavior as a disciple of Jesus Christ. Are you living up to the call of discipleship as he has described it? Where could you do better? How could you, as busy as your life is, live it more completely for God? Are your priorities where they need to be or are you too often thinking in terms of earthly things and not things heavenly? Amen.

Proper 20
Pentecost 17
Ordinary Time 25
Mark 9:30-37

They went on from there and passed through Galilee. He did not want anyone to know it; for he was teaching his disciples, saying to them, "The Son of Man is to be betrayed into human hands, and they will kill him, and three days after being killed, he will rise again." But they did not understand what he was saying and were afraid to ask him. Then they came to Capernaum; and when he was in the house he asked them, "What were you arguing about on the way?" But they were silent, for on the way they had argued with one another who was the greatest. He sat down, called the twelve, and said to them, "Whoever wants to be first must be last of all and servant of all." Then he took a little child and put it among them; and taking it in his arms, he said to them, "Whoever welcomes one such child in my name welcomes me, and whoever welcomes me welcomes not me but the one who sent me."

Speaking Truth to Power
and Hope to the Powerless

Let's get this story straight; Jesus and his disciples were making their way to the town of Capernaum, and as they were walking along three things happened: First, Jesus told his disciples that things were going to go down hill in a big hurry, that he would be betrayed, killed, but three days later, he would rise again. That's the first thing that happened.

The second thing that was going on was that the disciples didn't understand what in the world he meant, and they were afraid to ask him. It makes sense. They had been with Jesus for some time now and still there were occasions when he seemed to be speaking a different language. They weren't able to grasp what he was trying to teach them. And, probably, they were also scared a bit about what betrayal and killing and rising might mean for *them*, not just Jesus.

Well, the third thing was that the disciples changed the subject and began to argue about which one of them was the greatest. They didn't understand and perhaps didn't want to understand what Jesus was talking about and so they talked about something different — which one of them is the greatest, the top dog, the big kahuna. Whose polling numbers were going up and whose numbers were going down? We can hardly blame them. There are probably not many of us here who haven't, at one time or other, dreamed of a little fame, recognition, or even glory. To fantasize like this is a good way to get our minds off of other, more difficult subjects.

When I was a young boy and just learning guitar, I think I probably knew four chords at the time, I attended a Bobby Vinton Concert. Pardon me for showing my age and referencing someone only spoken of in *Trivial Pursuit* or on *Jeopardy*. Please feel free to pull out your smart phones and Google "Bobby Vinton."

My band mates and I (who also knew only four chords, and maybe three songs, even though the majority of songs that were popular at the time could be played with those same few chords) were sitting in the first row off to the side watching the roadies set up. It looked to me like one guitarist was missing and I began to think that maybe they would have a call out for someone to take his place. That would sure move me up the scale of importance at my high school if they called on me. I wouldn't just be the skinny kid, yeah… just try to imagine *that*, the skinny kid with a tuba and an out-of-tune guitar. I would have been on the stage with a national recording artist.

Sadly, but in the end, thankfully, the guitarist arrived and I was spared the humiliation. I don't think I was then, or now much different from a lot of people. Look at the preponderance of TV shows where people of great talent as well as those of dubious talent and sound mental health, strive to be the greatest, and achieve the fame and fortune they've been dreaming about all their lives. Or the countless so-called reality shows, which do not show anything that resembles the reality I live in, where people will do anything, *anything*, to win, to show that they are the best, the greatest. Nope, we are a lot alike I suspect and very much like the disciples.

Imagine that you are daydreaming about being famous,

or rich, or the best, and someone asks you what you're thinking about. *A penny for your thoughts.* Your response might be, *Oh, nothing, just daydreaming.* We might be embarrassed to tell the truth. It appears that this was the case for the disciples, and when Jesus asked them what they were chatting about on the road, they were silent.

So Jesus called the twelve disciples together and taught them a lesson that he had been trying to teach them for some time: If you want to be first then you have to be last of all, and servant of all (Mark 9:35). No doubt that was not what they wanted to hear. But they were silent. So Jesus decided that an object lesson was in order.

He took a little child and stood her in their midst and took her in his arms and told them that whoever welcomes one such child in his name welcomes him, and whoever welcomes him actually is welcoming the Father who sent him. Now it may look like Jesus had given up trying to teach the disciples and changed the subject, but I don't believe he had. Think about who in the ancient world, and probably in our world as well, have the least amount of power. Children in those days got little respect, for the most part they didn't count, they had no legal status and didn't do anything productive. In short, children were on the bottom rung of society, but not for Jesus and his upside-down world. Later in this gospel we'll see the disciples shooing children away from Jesus. And Jesus became irate.

So Jesus put one of these little ones, the least of all in society, in the midst of the disciples and said, in effect, the only way you can have any importance in the kingdom of God is to care for, to welcome, to serve those who are least of all. The only way that the disciples can be reckoned as having any status whatsoever is for them to serve the powerless. It is a theme we hear over and over in the gospels, the first must be last of all and servants of all, the last will be first and the first shall be last.

We've heard it over and over from Jesus but we also have heard, over and over in our daily lives, the opposite: the first shall be first, the powerful shall have power over those who have less power.

Perhaps it is difficult to remember that the call to be a disciple of Jesus means putting our own ambitions in perspective, except for the ambition to care for those who are least of all, who are unable to care for themselves, who slip through the cracks constantly; the children and other powerless ones in our society.

I have to admit that this seems to go against the grain sometimes and that we can come up with all sorts of reasons why some of those powerless ones have more power than they appear to have and so need to do for themselves instead of having others do for them. I get it. Yes, there are those who are fully capable of caring for themselves and their families and still they have their hand out. I'm not talking about them and I'm quite sure that Jesus is not talking about them either.

I just ask that we look first at ourselves and recognize the power that each of us has, and the responsibility according to the gospel of Jesus Christ, to use our power and vast resources to make life better for the powerless. It is what Jesus was trying to teach his disciples and teach us today. Amen.

Proper 21
Pentecost 18
Ordinary Time 26
Mark 9:38-50

John said to him, "Teacher, we saw someone casting out demons in your name, and we tried to stop him, because he was not following us." But Jesus said, "Do not stop him; for no one who does a deed of power in my name will be able soon afterward to speak evil of me. Whoever is not against us is for us. For truly I tell you, whoever gives you a cup of water to drink because you bear the name of Christ will by no means lose the reward. "If any of you put a stumbling block before one of these little ones who believe in me, it would be better for you if a great millstone were hung around your neck and you were thrown into the sea. If your hand causes you to stumble, cut it off; it is better for you to enter life maimed than to have two hands and to go to hell, to the unquenchable fire. And if your foot causes you to stumble, cut it off; it is better for you to enter life lame than to have two feet and to be thrown into hell. And if your eye causes you to stumble, tear it out; it is better for you to enter the kingdom of God with one eye than to have two eyes and to be thrown into hell, where their worm never dies, and the fire is never quenched. For everyone will be salted with fire. Salt is good; but if salt has lost its saltiness, how can you season it? Have salt in yourselves, and be at peace with one another."

Gouge-Your-Eye-Out Sunday

There are a couple of Sundays I'd just as soon not preach. One is Trinity Sunday, the Sunday immediately following Pentecost. I've heard more than one priest say that the reason most of us want an assistant or a deacon is so that we can assign them the task of trying to explain how it is we believe in one God, in three persons, and so on. Clergy dislike of preaching on Trinity Sunday is pretty widespread. So-called, Stewardship Sunday is another. It feels to me like I'm singing for my supper. After all, besides the mortgage what costs a church the most? Clergy salaries. Plus, I can guarantee you that regardless of how many guests a church has had in the weeks leading up to Stewardship Sunday, there will be several that day and it will be the greeter's job to assure them that we don't talk about money every Sunday. So I tread carefully on those Sundays. By the way, that Sunday is coming up in a couple of weeks. Beware!

There are others but let me get right to the point. The most dreaded Sunday, for me is today, the day that one of our parishioners so pointedly calls: *Gouge-Your-Eye-Out Sunday*. The other day we were discussing which Sunday would be best for a kind of invite-a-friend-to-church Sunday, and she said, any Sunday except *Gouge-Your-Eye-Out Sunday*. She understood why I'd prefer not to preach today. But, as I've said many times before when difficult readings come up, I don't pick them. Some bunches of people many years ago arranged the series of Sunday readings we call the lectionary and this just happens to be the day they picked for *cut-your-hand-off, cut-your-foot-off, gouge-your-eye-out Sunday*. So, these are the cards we've been dealt, let's see where they take us this morning.

I think it's safe to say that Jesus is serious about sin. To put it mildly, he stressed that sin was a bad idea. To put it bluntly, he thought that it would be better for us to go through life without one or more appendages than to sin, and especially, to cause someone who believes in him to sin. That, I believe, is a given. Jesus hated sin. I also think it's safe to say that most and maybe all those who have read and studied this passage understand that Jesus was not expecting anyone to take it literally. Even the most literal of scriptural interpreters, those whose bumper sticker might read, *God said it, I believe it, that's the end of it*; have yet to pluck out an eye or amputate an arm or a leg. And it's not because their eyes or arms or legs have not caused them to sin, for as Saint Paul says, "[Since] all have sinned and fall short of the glory of God they are now justified by his grace as a gift, through the redemption that is in Christ Jesus" (Romans 3:23-24).

Jesus was trying to make a point. He often spoke in vivid terms like these. In Luke's gospel it is recorded that he said, "Whoever comes to me and does not hate father and mother, wife and children, brothers and sister, yes, and even life itself, cannot be my disciple" (Luke 14:26). Certainly Jesus knew that there was quite enough hatred in the world already and did not intend for his followers to add to it, yet he spoke in such a striking way so as to help us realize that sometime down the line we may be forced to make very difficult decisions about who or what to follow.

Or when Jesus told the rich young man to sell everything he has and give it to the poor if he wanted to have treasure in heaven, or when he told his disciples regarding this man, that it is hard for those who have wealth to enter the kingdom of God. Jesus was trying to make a point. A point we'll be exploring in two weeks, by the way.

To be sure, we need to be on guard and not dilute these sayings of Jesus, and turn eye gouging and limb amputation into a hand slap and don't do that again or give all we have to the poor and then follow Jesus to mean, give whatever is left over at the end of the month to God and God's work.

Jesus spoke the way he did, I believe, to get our attention, to wake us up, to force us to examine our behavior and not take the easy way out.

He spoke this way so that perhaps we might catch ourselves when we too casually dismiss his statements about sin and discipleship as simply the way Middle Easterners talked back then.

He spoke this way, I believe, so that these words of his might stick to us, not easily be forgotten, but instead cause us to carefully look at the life we are living to judge for ourselves whether or not we stack up; whether we can legitimately count ourselves as disciples of Jesus Christ.

How might Jesus speak today? What kinds of images might he use? I wonder. Perhaps it would be something like this: If your use of the internet caused you to surf where you know you had no business going, unplug your computer, smash it with a sledge hammer, and toss it in the city dump.

If in your use of Facebook you find your self searching for long-lost boyfriends or girlfriends, drawing you further away from your spouse or partner, stop using the service and never go back again.

If your love of possessions causes you to judge those who have less than you or to be envious of others who have more than you, or put things before people, get rid of what you own; your beautiful house, your fancy car, your membership at the country club, and give the money to the poor and follow Jesus. You get the idea. Actually, I think Jesus would use far more colorful images than these but it's the best I could do.

Some time ago I was having a discussion with a pastor from a different franchise and he was asking why I was so rigid about following the lectionary. My response was simple: If I didn't, if I picked and chose passages myself based on the ones I liked, or the ones I thought my congregation needed to hear and pay attention to, my tendency would be to skip over the tough ones, the ones that called *my* lifestyle into question, or the ones that might cause my congregation not to like me because of something I felt compelled to preach based on the scripture. I told him, I feel it is best to take my chances, let the pericopes fall where they may, and then preach the gospel as best I can, with, as Saint Paul says in his letter to the church in Philipi, "to work out my own salvation with fear and trembling" (Philippians 2:12c paraphrased).

So what are we to do with all of this? How are we to respond to Jesus who is speaking so harshly and so loudly to us about sin and the need to avoid sin and especially not to lead others into sin? I think we should not take his words lightly. We should not dismiss them out-of-hand. Hear them as, in the best sense, a cry for attention, and as a message across the ages that is saying to us that there are ways to behave that bring us closer to God and God's promises, and ways to live that take us further away. There is a way to live in community so that everyone can thrive and grow closer to each other and to God and hear Jesus' words as a call to live a holy and wholesome life.

Let's face it; we all know what sin is. We all know when

we stray, when we fall short, when we begin to rationalize our behavior. We know, don't we? May these words of Jesus remind us every day of the path he expects us to take, the path he bids us to walk, this day and always, forever and ever. Amen.

Proper 22
Pentecost 19
Ordinary Time 27
Mark 10:2-16

Some Pharisees came, and to test him they asked, "Is it lawful for a man to divorce his wife?" He answered them, "What did Moses command you?" They said, "Moses allowed a man to write a certificate of dismissal and to divorce her." But Jesus said to them, "Because of your hardness of heart he wrote this commandment for you. But from the beginning of creation, 'God made them male and female.' 'For this reason a man shall leave his father and mother and be joined to his wife, and the two shall become one flesh.' So they are no longer two, but one flesh. Therefore what God has joined together, let no one separate." Then in the house the disciples asked him again about this matter. He said to them, "Whoever divorces his wife and marries another commits adultery against her; and if she divorces her husband and marries another, she commits adultery." People were bringing little children to him in order that he might touch them; and the disciples spoke sternly to them. But when Jesus saw this, he was indignant and said to them, "Let the little children come to me; do not stop them; for it is to such as these that the kingdom of God belongs. Truly I tell you, whoever does not receive the kingdom of God as a little child will never enter it." And he took them up in his arms, laid his hands on them, and blessed them.

And They Lived Happily Ever After... or Did They?

This is a story I tell from time to time at weddings. It's based on a Moroccan folktale.[1]

Once upon a time there was a much beloved king who was so rich that he measured his wealth in bushel baskets. Sadly, his wealth did not prevent him from contracting a fatal illness and in time the man lay on his deathbed. He called his only son to his side and said, "Son, you are all I have left. Your mother is gone, you have no brothers or sisters, and so in a short time you will become king. Besides my hope that you will rule our people with kindness and love, I need you to promise me one thing."

"Anything Father," the son said.

"After I am gone, and you become king there will come a time when you will want to marry. At that time I want you to promise me that you will ask your very best friend in all the world to go throughout the kingdom and even the entire world if necessary in order to find the woman that God intends for you to marry. Will you promise me?"

"Yes, father. When the time comes I will ask my best friend to find for me the woman that God intends for me to marry."

Soon after the king died and the son assumed the throne. Though he was still quite young he was found to be a strong and capable leader. Though he was not loved by all, for no leader is, still he loved everyone and treated them with the same kindness and mercy that his father had shown them. Time passed and the young king in his twenties decided it was time to marry. He called his best friend to his side and asked him to search for the woman that God intended for him to marry.

In a short time word came back to the castle that the friend had found the woman that God intended for the king to marry and wedding preparations began. The friend brought the young woman to the bridal chamber. A heavy stone was placed at the door so that it could open only a little bit, not enough to admit the king. It was there as a test. If the young king could move the stone aside then this woman was the one that God intended for him. If he could not move the stone, then, sadly, she was not. When the king was told of her beauty, how upright and caring she was, he hurried up the stairs to the bridal chamber to sneak a peek!

Inside he saw the most stunning woman he had ever seen in his life. She was lovely, dressed in a gown, her hair braided and woven around her head. Quietly she hummed a tune that seemed familiar to him but he could not remember why. She was lighting the candles on a candelabra and as she grace-fully turned toward the door as she finished there is no other modern word to describe the king's feelings: he was *smitten*. Clearly she would be a suitable companion, his friend had succeeded, and she was the woman that God intended for him to marry. So he bent down and began to push against the stone. He pushed. He shoved. He grunted and groaned, but sadly, the stone would not move. This woman was not to be his wife; she was not the person that God intended for him to marry. Word went out and the wedding preparations were put on hold.

The best friend began his quest anew and within a few days another potential bride was found. She too was reported to be beautiful. A woman of fine character and of spotless reputation. With great joy wedding preparations resumed. She was brought to the bridal chamber and once again, a stone was rolled against the door. The young king dashed up the stairs to see his new bride. Through the crack in the door he saw an exotic woman. Her hair was teased, woven with ribbons and jewels and piled upon her head. Her clothes were the silks of a dancer. Throughout the room there were burning candles and incense. As she began to gently dance, tapping her foot, the tiny bells on her ankle jingled. She too began to hum a tune that was familiar to the man as she danced the age-old dance of a woman before a man. As their eyes met, passion filled his heart to make this woman his lover and bride. He thought to himself that his friend had outdone himself this time. So he leaned against the stone. He pushed and pulled but the stone would not move. Again he grunted and groaned but no, the stone would not budge. It became clear to him that this was not the woman that God intended for him. That did not, however, keep him from taking one more look at this exotic and beautiful woman!

Again the search resumed. It was a few weeks later when the best friend announced the she had been found and secretly brought to the bridal chambers, the door again secured with the stone.

Wedding preparations were nearly complete. This time the young king did not approach the bridal chamber quite so eagerly. He stood there, eyed the stubborn stone and peeked inside. There he saw a simple maiden, a woman from the village dressed as a peasant, her long hair cascading onto her shoulders. She was sitting in a rocking chair, next to a table with a single candle, a quilt on her lap. As she sewed she began to sing a song, *that* song, a song so familiar. He remembered it from his childhood. He also began to remember *her*, running through fields, flowers in hand, climbing trees, sharing their dreams with each other. Truly this was a friend whom God intended for him to marry. He stepped back, looked warily at the obstinate stone, put his hands to the task and pushed, and struggled, and grunted and groaned… but it would not move. The woman continued to sing, and rock, and sew.

Suddenly he realized that the tune *she* was singing was the same one that the first woman had hummed, and the second had danced to. All three were the same woman; she would be his companion, his lover, and his friend. If only the stupid stone would move! He pushed harder.

Nothing. He was about to give up when he heard a voice, her voice, through the crack in the door, "Here, let me help you move the stone." She reached through the crack, they put their hands together and the stone moved easily aside. The bells rang; the celebration began, the couple married, for the king had found the woman that God intended for him. And she had found the man that God intended for her as well.

At this point, at weddings I stop and ask the congregation how this story should end. If I say to them: *And the king and his bride lived…* the congregation always responds with, *happily ever after.* And I say, *No. You know better. You all know that in the midst of life there are always stones placed in our paths and one of the wonders of marriage is that there are now two people to put their hands and their shoulders and their hearts to these stones to move them out of the way.* And since the congregation has promised to do all in their power to support this couple on their journey, I remind them of their responsibility to be there when the stones get too big, or too frequent, and help move them out of the way.

This week, when you think of this story, tell it to yourself in order to work your way back to this one simple point. Jesus is responding to a question that is based on a law in the book of Deuteronomy that states that a man can write a certificate of divorce if the woman he marries does not *please* him. I think Jesus is saying to them and to us in the gospel, in his very clear way, that marriage is not something, as our prayer book states, to be entered into unadvisedly or lightly. It is not something that you walk away from if your partner *does not please you.* He is saying that there will be struggles and hardships in any relationship, but that the couple must work together to overcome them, and if that fails, to call upon the community to lend a hand, to help them do what they could not do alone; the vows made in marriage are to be kept as far as it is humanly possible. Dissolving those promises should be only done as a last resort, after all attempts to move the obstacles aside have been made by the couple with the help of the community. May all couples everywhere have the grace and perseverance to keep the promises they made today, tomorrow, and forever and ever. Amen.

---

1. This story is based on a Moroccan folktale as told by Elrbarry at the wedding of his daughter. www.eldrbarry.net/marriage/stondoor.htm.

www.ingramcontent.com/pod-product-compliance
Lightning Source LLC
LaVergne TN
LVHW021118080426
835509LV00021B/3436